For exams from September 2025 to December 2026

ICAEW
Accounting Fundamentals

First edition 2025

ISBN 9781 0355 3079 3

eISBN 9781 0355 2951 3

British Library Cataloguing-in-Publication Data

A catalogue record for this publication is available from the British Library

Published by

BPP Learning Media Ltd
BPP House, Aldine Place
142-144 Uxbridge Road
London W12 8AA

learningmedia.bpp.com

Printed in the United Kingdom

Your learning materials, published by BPP Learning Media Ltd, are printed on paper obtained from traceable sustainable sources.

All rights reserved. No part of this publication may be reproduced, stored in a retrieval system or transmitted, in any form or by any means, electronic, mechanical, photocopying, recording or otherwise, without the prior written permission of BPP Learning Media.

NO AI TRAINING. Unless otherwise agreed in writing, the use of BPP material for the purpose of AI training is not permitted. Any use of this material to "train" generative artificial intelligence (AI) technologies is prohibited, as is providing archived or cached data sets containing such material to another person or entity.

The content of this publication is intended to prepare students for the ICAEW examinations, and should not be used as professional advice. Although every effort has been made to ensure that the contents of this book are correct at the time of going to press, BPP Learning Media makes no warranty that the information in this book is accurate or complete and accepts no liability for any loss or damage suffered by any person acting or refraining from acting as a result of the material in this book.

ICAEW takes no responsibility for the content of any supplemental training materials supplied by the Partner in Learning.

The ICAEW Partner in Learning logo, ACA and ICAEW CFAB are all registered trademarks of ICAEW and are used under licence by BPP Learning Media Ltd.

©

BPP Learning Media Ltd

BPP Learning Media is grateful to the IASB for permission to reproduce extracts from IFRS® Accounting Standards, IAS® Standards, SIC and IFRIC. This publication contains copyright © material and trademarks of the IFRS Foundation®. All rights reserved. Used under license from the IFRS Foundation®. Reproduction and use rights are strictly limited. For more information about the IFRS Foundation and rights to use its material please visit www.IFRS.org.

Disclaimer: To the extent permitted by applicable law the Board and the IFRS Foundation expressly disclaims all liability howsoever arising from this publication or any translation thereof whether in contract, tort or otherwise (including, but not limited to, liability for any negligent act or omission) to any person in respect of any claims or losses of any nature including direct, indirect, incidental or consequential loss, punitive damages, penalties or cost.

Information contained in this publication does not constitute advice and should not be substituted for the services of an appropriately qualified professional.

Copyright © IFRS Foundation

All rights reserved. Reproduction and use rights are strictly limited. No part of this publication may be translated, reprinted or reproduced or utilised in any form either in whole or in part or by any electronic, mechanical or other means, now known or hereafter invented, including photocopying and recording, or in any information storage and retrieval system, without prior permission in writing from the IFRS Foundation. Contact the IFRS Foundation for further details.

The Foundation has trade marks registered around the world (Trade Marks) including 'IAS®', 'IASB®', 'IFRIC®', 'IFRS®', the IFRS® logo, 'IFRS for SMEs®', IFRS for SMEs® logo, the 'Hexagon Device', 'International Financial Reporting Standards®', NIIF® and 'SIC®'.

Further details of the Foundation's Trade Marks are available from the Licensor on request.

| Preface | Contents |

Welcome to BPP Learning Media's **Passcards** for ICAEW **Accounting Fundamentals**.

- They **save you time**. Important topics are summarised for you.
- They incorporate **diagrams** to kick start your memory.
- They follow the overall **structure** of the ICAEW Workbook, but BPP Learning Media's ICAEW **Passcards** are not just a condensed book. Each card has been separately designed for clear presentation. Topics are self-contained and can be grasped visually.
- ICAEW **Passcards** are **just the right size** for pockets, briefcases and bags.
- ICAEW **Passcards focus on the exams** you will be facing.

Run through the **Passcards** as often as you can during your final revision period. The day before the exam, try to go through the **Passcards** again! You will then be well on your way to passing your exams.

Good luck!

		Page			Page
1	Introduction to accounting	1	8	Irrecoverable debts and allowances for receivables	65
2	The accounting equation	15	9	Accruals and prepayments	69
3	Recording financial transactions	21	10	Non-current assets and depreciation	73
4	Ledger accounting and double entry	27	11	Company financial statements	81
5	Preparing basic financial statements	37	12	Company financial statements under IFRS Accounting Standards	91
6	Errors and corrections to accounting records and financial statements	47	13	Company financial statements under UK GAAP	97
7	Cost of sales and inventories	57	14	Sole trader and partnerships under UK GAAP	105

Notes

1: Introduction to accounting

Topic List

- The purpose of accounting information
- The regulation of accounting
- Sustainability and sustainability standards
- The main financial statements
- Capital and revenue items
- Qualitative characteristics of useful accounting information
- Accounting concepts and conventions
- Ethical considerations

This chapter looks at why financial statements are prepared and how accounting information is used.

We review the regulatory environment and the need for an ethical underpinning. We will also look at the development of sustainability disclosure standards, which is a major development in the profession.

We will introduce the primary financial statements and consider the main accounting concepts and conventions on which financial statements are based. Ethical considerations are introduced, with a focus on the fundamental principles. We will also look at the distinction between capital and revenue expenditure.

| The purpose of accounting information | The regulation of accounting | Sustainability and sustainability standards | The main financial statements | Capital and revenue items |

Accounting is a way of recording, analysing and summarising the transactions of an entity.

There are three main types of profit-making business entity

Sole trader
The sole trader owns his or her own business. They may have employees.

Partnership
Two or more people may go into business together, sharing risks and rewards. Examples are accounting firms, solicitors, dentists.

Limited liability company
Limited liability companies are owned by their shareholders and managed by directors. The company itself is a separate legal entity.

Who needs financial information?

In the case of limited liability companies, especially listed companies, there is a wide group of users.

Users of accounts

- Managers of the company
- Shareholders of the company
- Trade contacts
- Providers of finance to the company
- Taxation authorities (HMRC)
- Employees of the company
- Financial analysts and advisors
- Government and their agencies
- The public

The larger the entity, the greater the interest from various groups of people.

User information needs:

- Users need information in order to make decisions relating to providing resources to an entity

Users need to assess:

- The resources of an entity, claims against those resources and changes in the resources and claims
- How efficiently and effectively management have discharged their responsibilities
- The sustainability of an entity's operations and how an entity contributes to society

| The purpose of accounting information | **The regulation of accounting** | Sustainability and sustainability standards | The main financial statements | Capital and revenue items |

Influences upon financial accounting

Ethical standards
IESBA Code of Ethics
ICAEW Code of Ethics

National law
Form and content of accounts may be regulated by national legislation.

Accounting standards
The IASB produces IFRS Accounting Standards. The IFRS Advisory Committee and IFRS Interpretations Committee help tackle issues/interpretation of standards.

Accounting concepts and individual judgement

Sustainability disclosure standards
The ISSB has developed disclosure standards which focus on sustainability and climate-related matters.

GAAP
Drawn from:
- Local company law
- Accounting standards
- Statutory requirement in other countries
- Stock exchanges

Accounting standards

Developed at an international level by the IASB, they include:

- IFRS Accounting Standards
- IAS
- IFRIC Interpretations
- SIC interpretations

UK GAAP

Non-listed companies in the UK can choose IFRS Accounting Standards or UK Financial Reporting Standards (FRS). There are different IFRS Accounting Standards for different issues, but only one main accounting standard in the UK – FRS 102 – covering all issues.

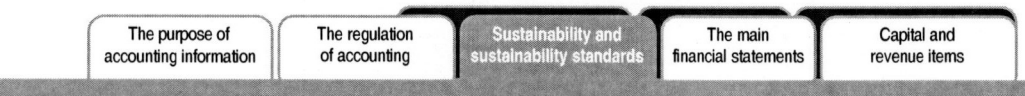

Information on sustainability is important to users in making decisions about providing resources to an entity and wider stakeholders.

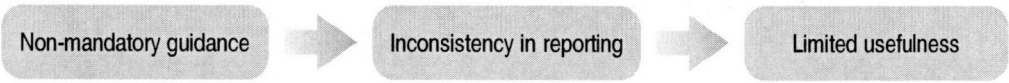

ISSB

ISSB aims to **provide high-quality, transparent and comparable information relating to sustainability** in the annual report.

ISSB focused on meeting the needs of primary users and capital markets.

Two standards issued:

- IFRS S1 General Requirements for Disclosure of Sustainability-related Financial Information
- IFRS S2 Climate-related Disclosures

Fundamental aspects to sustainability reporting:

Impacts Reporting on how a company positively or negatively affects environmental, societal, and governance issues eg worker rights, health and safety policy, waste, greenhouse gas emissions.

Dependencies Reporting on how environmental, societal and governance issues affect a company's financial statements and its ability to maintain value eg worker health, resource availability, regulation.

Information on dependencies is more useful to investors.

| The purpose of accounting information | The regulation of accounting | Sustainability and sustainability standards | **The main financial statements** | Capital and revenue items |

Main financial statements

Statement of financial position

A list of assets controlled by the entity and liabilities owed by the entity on a particular date.

- Total assets = Total liabilities + equity
- Amount invested by owner is **equity** (capital).

The statement shows the entity's **financial position** at a given point in time.

Statement of profit or loss

A record of income generated and expenditure incurred over a given period.

The statement of profit or loss shows the entity's **financial performance** over a period of time.

Financial statements must give a 'true and fair view' or 'present fairly' the entity's financial position.

| The purpose of accounting information | The regulation of accounting | Sustainability and sustainability standards | The main financial statements | **Capital and revenue items** |

Capital expenditure

This results in the acquisition of non-current assets, or an increase in their earning capacity.

Revenue expenditure

This is incurred for the purpose of trade or to maintain the existing earning capacity of the non-current assets.

Examples

- Property purchase
- Vehicle purchases
- Plant and machinery purchases
- Cost of installing plant and machinery

Examples

- Property repairs
- Depreciation of assets
- Computer maintenance
- Travel costs
- Office expenses

| Qualitative characteristics of useful accounting information | Accounting concepts and conventions | Ethical considerations |

The two fundamental qualitative characteristics defined by the *Conceptual Framework* are:

- Relevance – predictive or confirmatory value
- Faithful representation – complete, neutral (prudence), free from error

Relevant and faithfully represented information is enhanced by

- Timeliness
- Understandability
- Verifiability
- Comparability

| Qualitative characteristics of useful accounting information | Accounting concepts and conventions | Ethical considerations |

IAS 1, *Presentation of Financial Statements* considers accounting policies, fundamental assumptions and the format and content of financial statements.

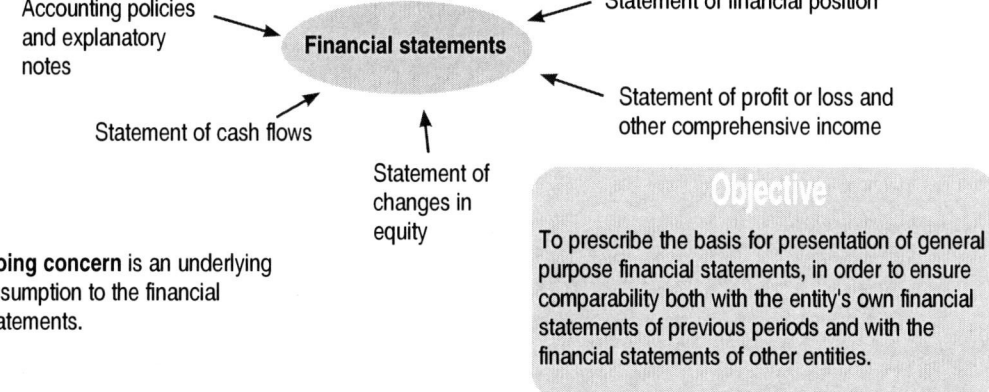

- Accounting policies and explanatory notes
- Statement of cash flows
- Statement of changes in equity
- Statement of financial position
- Statement of profit or loss and other comprehensive income

Going concern is an underlying assumption to the financial statements.

Objective

To prescribe the basis for presentation of general purpose financial statements, in order to ensure comparability both with the entity's own financial statements of previous periods and with the financial statements of other entities.

| Qualitative characteristics of useful accounting information | **Accounting concepts and conventions** | Ethical considerations |

Financial statements should **present fairly** financial performance, financial position and cash flows. Compliance with IFRS Accounting Standards will help to ensure this.

Going concern
The entity will continue in operation for the foreseeable future. There is no intention to put the entity into liquidation or to make drastic cutbacks to the scale of the operations.

Accruals
Revenue and costs must be recognised as they are earned or incurred, not as money is received or paid. They must be matched with one another and dealt with in the period in which they are incurred.

Business entity
The entity is separate from its assets.

Consistency
The presentation and classification of items should stay the same from one period to the next.

Materiality
Information is material if omitting, misstating or obscuring it could influence the economic decisions of users.

Historical cost
Transactions are recorded at the cost when they occurred.

| Qualitative characteristics of useful accounting information | Accounting concepts and conventions | **Ethical considerations** |

Judgement is required in applying accounting concepts.

The exercise of judgement in accounting matters should always be underpinned by **ethical principles**.

IESBA Code of Ethics for Professional Accountants

- **Integrity** – straightforward and honest in all relationships.
- **Objectivity** – do not allow bias, conflict of interest or undue influence of others to override judgements.
- **Professional competence and due care** – duty to maintain professional knowledge and skill, act diligently and in accordance with applicable standards.
- **Confidentiality** – respect the confidentiality of information acquired.
- **Professional behaviour** – comply with relevant laws and regulations and avoid any action that discredits the profession.

ICAEW Code of Ethics is a principles-based system.

Notes

2: The accounting equation

Topic List

The accounting equation

Credit transactions

The statement of financial position

The statement of profit or loss

This chapter looks at the fundamental mechanics of financial statements and introduces the statement of financial position and statement of profit or loss.

The accounting equation will help you to see why the statement of financial position must balance.

	The accounting equation	Credit transactions	The statement of financial position	The statement of profit or loss

Basic Accounting Equation

ASSETS = CAPITAL + LIABILITIES

Extended Accounting Equation

ASSETS = CAPITAL + PROFITS - DRAWINGS + LIABILITIES

Capital
Investment of funds with the intention of earning a return

Profits
Excess of income over expenses

Drawings
Amounts withdrawn from the owner of the business

| | The accounting equation | **Credit transactions** | The statement of financial position | The statement of profit or loss |

Credit transactions mean there is a timing difference between when purchases and sales are undertaken and when cash is received. These give rise to:

Trade receivable

An asset: a balance owed to the business by a credit customer

A credit customer is also known as a **debtor**.

Trade payable

A liability: a balance owed by the business to a credit supplier

A credit supplier is also known as a **creditor**.

| | The accounting equation | Credit transactions | **The statement of financial position** | The statement of profit or loss |

The statement of financial position

A list of assets, liabilities and capital of a business at a given moment.

Happiness
Statement of financial position
as at 31 August 20X1

ASSETS	£	£
Non-current assets		
Land and buildings		100,000
Fixtures and fittings		16,000
Motor vehicles		18,000
		134,000
Current assets		
Inventories	10,000	
Trade receivables	23,000	
Prepayments	100	
Cash	700	
		33,800
Total assets		167,800

Non-current assets are acquired for continuing use within the business for a period of more than one year.

Current assets are cash or assets that are expected to be converted into cash within one year.

EQUITY AND LIABILITIES		
Equity		
Capital as at 1 September 20X0		95,200
Profit for the year		16,000
		111,200
Less drawings		(8,000)
Capital as at 31 August 20X1		103,200
Non-current liabilities		
Loan		50,000
Current liabilities		
Bank overdraft	4,000	
Trade payables	3,600	
Taxation payable	7,000	
		14,600
		167,800

Non-current liabilities are payable after more than one year.

Current liabilities are payable within one year.

Capital + liabilities = assets

| The accounting equation | Credit transactions | The statement of financial position | **The statement of profit or loss** |

The statement of profit or loss

This matches revenue earned in a period with the costs incurred in earning it.

This is known as the **accruals concept**.

Gross profit = revenue − cost of sales

Profit for the year = gross profit − expenses

Happiness – Statement of profit or loss for the year ended 31 August 20X1

	£	£
Revenue		80,000
Opening inventory	5,000	
Purchases	40,000	
Closing inventory	(10,000)	
Cost of goods sold		35,000
Gross profit		45,000
Less expenses		
Rent	12,000	
Depreciation	1,000	
Wages	12,000	
Other expenses	4,000	
		29,000
Profit for the year		**16,000**

3: Recording financial transactions

Topic List

Computerised accounting systems

Source documents for recording financial transactions

Recording bank transactions

The payroll

This chapter covers the main sources of data and will consider how computerised accounting systems are used to capture that data.

We will see how the data is recorded in the accounting records to reflect business transactions.

| **Computerised accounting systems** | Source documents for recording financial transactions | Recording bank transactions | The payroll |

- Computerised accounting systems are commonplace in most businesses.

Inputs → **Processes** → **Outputs**

- Source documents
- Standing data

- Ledgers
- Journals
- Calculations
- Record keeping

- Reports
- Trial balance
- Financial statements

- Software packages consist of 'ledgers' which capture the accounting information from the transactions businesses undertake.
- Cloud accounting allows a business to access accounting records via the internet.
- Assume a computerised accounting system is used, but you will need to consider the underlying principles and approach of a manual system to understand how a computerised system operates.

| Computerised accounting systems | **Source documents for recording financial transactions** | Recording bank transactions | The payroll |

Source documents

Business transactions are nearly always evidenced by a document. These documents are the source of the information in the accounts. Source documents you will see in *Accounting Fundamentals* are:

- Invoices (sales and purchases)
- Credit notes
- The bank transaction report

| Computerised accounting systems | Source documents for recording financial transactions | **Recording bank transactions** | The payroll |

Businesses have constant access to online banking and will use bank information to update accounting records. Computerised accounting systems can match transactions in the electronic bank statements to transactions in the accounting system.

Bank statement balance		Accounting system	Match	
Deposit	Withdrawal			Matches to transactions – system can suggest or manual
£650		Sales invoice 001 customer ABC £650	✓	Once matched, accounting system processes to correct ledger account
	(£900)	Purchase invoice supplier XYZ £900	✓	
	(£1,220)	Purchase invoice supplier JKL £1,300	✗	Unmatched items require investigation. Accountant discovers that prompt payment discount taken hence amount paid is less than invoice

| Computerised accounting systems | Source documents for recording financial transactions | Recording bank transactions | **The payroll** |

Payroll

Wages and salaries costs are entered into the accounting system from the payroll.

Payroll amounts break down as follows:

	£
Employee's gross pay	X
Employee's NI contribution	(X)
PAYE income tax	(X)
Employee's pension contribution	(X)
Balance paid to employee (net pay)	X

The employer will pay to HMRC:

	£
Employee's NI contribution	X
PAYE income tax	X
Plus employer's NI contribution	X
	X

Notes

4: Ledger accounting and double entry

Topic List

The nominal ledger

Double entry bookkeeping

Journal entries

The receivables and payables ledgers

Accounting for discounts

Accounting for VAT

This chapter looks at ledger accounting.

Information from source documents is recorded in ledger accounts. We will refer to the nominal ledger, the receivables ledger and the payables ledger. Transactions are recorded in the nominal ledger using double-entry bookkeeping.

VAT is a consumer expenditure tax.

| The nominal ledger | Double entry bookkeeping | Journal entries | The receivables and payables ledgers | Accounting for discounts | Accounting for VAT |

Ledger accounting

The process by which a business keeps a record of its transactions:

- In chronological order
- Built up in cumulative totals

A ledger account or 'T' account looks like this.

NAME OF ACCOUNT

£	£
DEBIT SIDE	CREDIT SIDE

The nominal ledger

The main accounting record in which accounting transactions are recorded. Accounts within the nominal ledger include the following.

- Plant and machinery (non-current asset)
- Inventories (current asset)
- Sales (income)
- Rent (expense)
- Trade payables (current liability)

| The nominal ledger | **Double entry bookkeeping** | Journal entries | The receivables and payables ledgers | Accounting for discounts | Accounting for VAT |

Basic principles: dual effect

Double entry bookkeeping is based on the same idea as the accounting equation.

- Every accounting transaction has two equal but opposite effects.
- Equality of assets and liabilities is preserved.

In a system of double entry bookkeeping every accounting event must be entered in ledger accounts both as a debit and as an equal but opposite credit.

Debit
- An increase in an expense
- An increase in an asset
- A decrease in a liability

Credit
- An increase in income
- An increase in a liability
- A decrease in an asset

Double entry bookkeeping

The rules of double entry bookkeeping are best learnt by considering the cash at bank account.

- A **credit** entry indicates a payment made by the business; the matching debit entry is then made in an account denoting an expense paid, an asset purchased or a liability settled.
- A **debit** entry in the cash at bank account indicates cash received by the business; the matching credit entry is then made in an account denoting revenue received, a liability created or an asset realised.

4: Ledger accounting and double entry

| The nominal ledger | Double entry bookkeeping | **Journal entries** | The receivables and payables ledgers | Accounting for discounts | Accounting for VAT |

Journal entry

Format of journal entries is as follows.

Date	Debit	Credit
	£	£
DEBIT A/c to be debited	X	
CREDIT A/c to be credited		X

Narrative to explain transaction

| The nominal ledger | Double entry bookkeeping | Journal entries | **The receivables and payables ledgers** | Accounting for discounts | Accounting for VAT |

The receivables and payables ledgers

To keep track of individual customer and supplier balances, it is common to maintain memorandum ledgers called the receivables ledger and the payables ledger. Each account in the receivables ledger represents the balance owed by an individual customer. Each account in the payables ledger represents the balance owed to an individual supplier.

Note that these receivables and payables ledgers **do not form part of the double entry system.**

In a computerised accounting system, the receivables ledger and the payables ledger are updated automatically when an entry is made against trade receivables or trade payables in the nominal ledger.

It is therefore very unlikely that there will be differences between the individual ledgers and the nominal ledger balances.

| The nominal ledger | Double entry bookkeeping | Journal entries | The receivables and payables ledgers | **Accounting for discounts** | Accounting for VAT |

Discounts

A discount is a reduction in the price of goods or services.

A supplier may have a **list** price at which it is prepared to provide its goods or services to the majority of customers. However, there may be reasons which justify a lower price or discount to particular customers or categories of customer.

It is useful to distinguish between two classes of discount:

- **Trade discount** is granted to regular customers, usually those buying in bulk quantities.
- **Early settlement discount** is granted to credit customers who pay within a specified period from the invoice date.

Accounting for early settlement discounts:

- Early settlement discounts offered to credit customers are deducted from revenue, either at the point of invoice (if the customer is expected to take advantage of the discount) or at the point of settlement of the invoice (if the customer was not originally expected to take advantage of the discount).
- Early settlement discounts received from credit suppliers are deducted from purchases either at the point of recording the invoice (if the company expects to take advantage of the discount) or at the point of payment of the invoice (if the company unexpectedly takes advantage of the discount).

Accounting for trade discounts:

- Trade discounts are deducted from revenue or purchases at the point of recording the invoice.

| The nominal ledger | Double entry bookkeeping | Journal entries | The receivables and payables ledgers | Accounting for discounts | **Accounting for VAT** |

VAT

An indirect tax levied on the sale of goods and services

- Administered by HMRC
- Can have a number of rates, eg, standard rate, reduced rate

Output VAT

Sales tax charged by the business on goods/services

Output greater than input? Pay difference to HMRC

Input greater than output? Refund due to business

Input VAT

Sales tax on purchases made by the business

| The nominal ledger | Double entry bookkeeping | Journal entries | The receivables and payables ledgers | Accounting for discounts | **Accounting for VAT** |

VAT and credit transactions

Sales

- Trade receivables balance includes VAT as it represents the total amount due to be received from customers.
- Sales are recorded net of (excluding VAT).
- VAT (output VAT) is recorded separately in the VAT account.

Purchases

- Trade payables balance includes VAT as it represents the total amount due to be paid to suppliers.
- Purchases are recorded net of (excluding) VAT.
- VAT (input VAT) is recorded separately in the VAT account.

Example

Trooper plc sold goods on credit to Lewis for £3,480 including VAT at 20%.

The journal entry to record the sale is:

DEBIT Trade receivables 3,480

CREDIT Revenue 2,900

CREDIT VAT 580

VAT and cash transactions

Sales

- The amount received will represent the goods sold plus the VAT collected. This should be recorded in the cash at bank account.
- Sales are recorded net of (excluding VAT).
- VAT (output VAT) is recorded separately in the VAT account.

Purchases

- The amount paid will represent the goods purchased plus the VAT paid on those goods. This should be recorded in the cash at bank account.
- Purchases are recorded net of (excluding) VAT.
- VAT (input VAT) is recorded separately in the VAT account.

Example

Trooper Ltd sold goods to Hardeep for £4,800 including VAT at 20%. Hardeep paid in cash at the point of sale.

The journal entry to record the cash sale is:

DEBIT	Cash at bank	4,800
CREDIT	Revenue	4,000
CREDIT	VAT	800

Notes

5: Preparing basic financial statements

Topic List

The trial balance

The statement of profit or loss

The statement of financial position

Preparing financial statements

Adjustments to the trial balance

The balances need to be extracted from the ledger accounts and entered into the trial balance.

Double entry bookkeeping dictates that the trial balance will have the same amount on the debit side as there is on the credit side.

| **The trial balance** | The statement of profit or loss | The statement of financial position | Preparing financial statements | Adjustments to the trial balance |

At the end of an accounting period a balance is struck on each ledger account.

- Total all debits and credits
- Debits exceed credits = debit balance
- Credits exceed debits = credit balance

An example of balancing a ledger account is shown below.

RECEIVABLES

	£		£
Sales	10,000	Cash	8,000
		Balance c/d	2,000
	10,000		10,000
Balance b/d	2,000		

Trial balance

The balances are then collected in a trial balance. Because every debit entry has an equal but opposite credit entry, total debits = total credits.

Errors

A trial balance does not guarantee accuracy. It will not pick up the following errors.

- Compensating errors
- Errors of commission
- Errors of omission
- Errors of principle

An example of a trial balance, incorporating the above receivables balance, is shown below.

ABC Traders
Trial balance as at 30 June 20X7

	£	£
Sales		35,000
Purchases	13,000	
Receivables	2,000	
Payables		1,500
Cash	10,000	
Capital		10,000
Loan		10,000
Rent	4,000	
Sundry expenses	3,500	
Loan interest paid	1,000	
Drawings	5,000	
Fixtures and fittings	18,000	
	56,500	56,500

| The trial balance | **The statement of profit or loss** | The statement of financial position | Preparing financial statements | Adjustments to the trial balance |

Balances on income and expense ledger accounts are NOT carried down to the next accounting period. Instead they are taken to the statement of profit or loss and the ledger accounts are cleared down to zero at the end of the period.

1. Prepare a proforma statement of profit or loss with income and expense lines included.

2. Transfer income and expense lines in the trial balance to the proforma.

3. Add down the statement of profit or loss to calculate the profit for the period.

Proforma statement of profit or loss

	£	£
ABC Traders		
Statement of profit or loss		
for the year ended 30 June 20X7		
Sales		35,000
Cost of sales (here = purchases)		13,000
Gross profit		22,000
Expenses		
Rent	4,000	
Sundry expenses	3,500	
Loan interest	1,000	
		8,500
Profit for the year		13,500

| The trial balance | The statement of profit or loss | **The statement of financial position** | Preparing financial statements | Adjustments to the trial balance |

Statement of financial position

The statement of financial position is prepared by following these steps:

1. Prepare a proforma statement of financial position with assets, liabilities and capital lines included
2. Transfer assets, liabilities, capital and drawings from the trial balance
3. Add profit for the year (from the statement of profit or loss) to capital
4. Add total assets. Add capital and liabilities. Check that total assets = total capital + liabilities

Prepare the statement as follows:

ABC Traders
Statement of financial position as at 30 June 20X7

	£	£
Non-current assets		
Fixtures and fittings		18,000
Current assets		
Receivables	2,000	
Cash at bank	10,000	
		12,000
		30,000
Proprietor's capital		18,500
Current liabilities		
Payables	1,500	
Loan	10,000	
		11,500
		30,000

| The trial balance | The statement of profit or loss | The statement of financial position | **Preparing financial statements** | Adjustments to the trial balance |

Accounting process overview

This diagram summarises the topics you have revised so far. Look at it just before your exam – everything should fall into place.

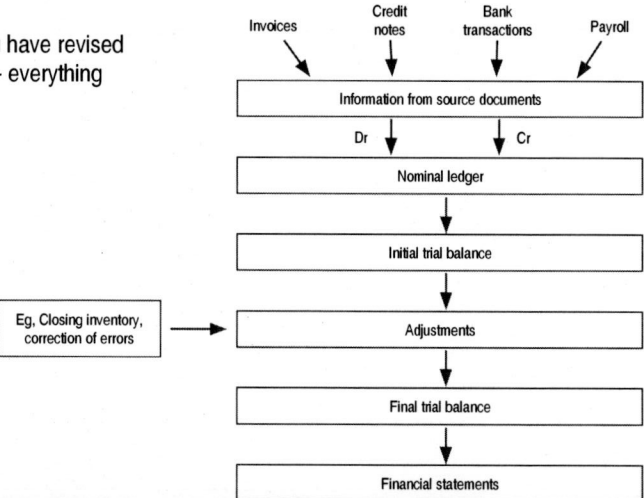

| The trial balance | The statement of profit or loss | The statement of financial position | Preparing financial statements | **Adjustments to the trial balance** |

Adjusting the trial balance

The initial trial balance may be adjusted for information that becomes known at or shortly after the year end or to correct errors.

The adjusted trial balance headings will look something like this.

Ledger account	Initial trial balance		Adjustments		Final trial balance	
	Dr	Cr	Dr	Cr	Dr	Cr
	£	£	£	£	£	£

| The trial balance | The statement of profit or loss | The statement of financial position | Preparing financial statements | **Adjustments to the trial balance** |

Process

1. Extract the initial trial balance from the accounting system.

2. Make the adjustments required:
   - Accruals and prepayments
   - Adjustments to inventory figures
   - Other adjustments (eg, depreciation and irrecoverable debts)

3. Check that any suspense a/c has been cleared.

4. Add the adjustments columns. Check the entries are correct and debits equal credits.

5. Add the figures across each line and record the total in the final trial balance columns.

6. Prepare the financial statements.

6: Errors and corrections to accounting records and financial statements

Topic List

Reconciliations

Types of error in accounting

The correction of errors

Suspense accounts

Trade receivables and trade payables record total amounts for all customers and suppliers. The receivables ledger and the payables ledger record the amounts owed from or to individual customers. In a computerised accounting system, the total for trade receivables will be equal to the total of the individual receivables ledger accounts at any point in time. The same is true of trade payables and the total of the payables ledger. A bank reconciliation will be carried out by a business on a regular, likely to be daily, basis. Any differences between the bank statement balance and the cash at bank balance need to be reconciled.

Although computerised systems are more accurate than manual systems, errors and omissions may still exist and require investigation and correction.

| Reconciliations | Types of error in accounting | The correction of errors | Suspense accounts |

Reconciliations

It is useful to check the accuracy of what is recorded in the nominal ledgers to external documents. The most common checks are:

Supplier statement reconciliations

Suppliers will regularly (monthly or quarterly) send a statement to a customer detailing the transactions in the period and the balance at the end of the period.

The business should reconcile the statements back to the payables memorandum accounts to ensure they are consistent.

Differences should be investigated.

Bank reconciliations – computerised accounting systems and electronic banking allow bank reconciliations to be performed at any point in time, usually daily.

Bank reconciliation

A comparison of a bank statement with the cash at bank account.

The bank reconciliation is an important financial control. The bank reconciliation will invariably show a difference.

Differences on bank reconciliation

Errors: more likely in the cash at bank account.

Omissions: items on the bank statement not in the cash at bank account (eg, bank charges). Omissions require correction using a journal entry.

Timing differences: eg, payments made and entered in the cash at bank account but not yet cleared through the bank.

| Reconciliations | Types of error in accounting | The correction of errors | Suspense accounts |

Proforma bank reconciliation

CASH AT BANK ACCOUNT

	£		£
Balance b/f	X	Dishonoured payment	X
Interest received	X	Bank charges	X
		Standing orders	X
		Direct debits	X
		Balance c/f	X
	X		X

	£
Balance per bank statement	X
Less uncleared payments	(X)
Plus uncleared receipts	X
Plus/less bank errors	X/(X)
Balance per adjusted cash at bank account	X

| Reconciliations | **Types of error in accounting** | The correction of errors | Suspense accounts |

Types of error

The main types of error are as follows

- Errors of transposition, eg, writing £381 as £318 (the difference is divisible by 9)
- Errors of omission, eg, receive supplier's invoice for £500 and do not record it in the accounts at all
- Errors of principle, eg, treating capital expenditure as revenue expenditure
- Errors of commission, eg, putting telephone expenses of £250 in the electricity expense account
- Compensating errors, eg, both sales and purchases coincidentally incorrect by £500

| Reconciliations | Types of error in accounting | **The correction of errors** | Suspense accounts |

Correction of errors

Errors can be corrected using a journal entry. Consider the following examples:

Example

Accountant omits to record invoice from supplier for £2,000. This would be corrected by the following journal entry:

DEBIT   Purchases   £2,000
CREDIT Payables   £2,000

A transaction previously omitted.

Example

Accountant posts car insurance of £800 to motor vehicles account. Correct as follows:

DEBIT   Motor expenses   £800
CREDIT Motor vehicles   £800

Correction of error of principle.

| Reconciliations | Types of error in accounting | The correction of errors | **Suspense accounts** |

A suspense account is a temporary account that is used in the following circumstances.

- The bookkeeper knows in which account to make the debit entry for a transaction but does not know where to make the corresponding credit entry (or vice versa).
- The credit is temporarily posted to the suspense account until the correct credit entry is known.

Any balance on a suspense account must be eliminated. It is **never** included in the final accounts.

Suspense account example

A business disposed of a machine which had a cost of £80,000 and a carrying amount at the date of disposal of £22,000. The bookkeeper recorded the proceeds of £16,000 in the bank but created a suspense account for the other side of the transaction.

What is the journal entry to remove the suspense account?

| | Reconciliations | Types of error in accounting | The correction of errors | **Suspense accounts** |

The bookkeeper should have recorded:

DEBIT	Bank	16,000	
DEBIT	Machinery accumulated depreciation	58,000	
DEBIT	Loss on disposal	6,000	
CREDIT	Machinery cost		80,000

The bookkeeper has recorded:

DEBIT	Bank	16,000	
CREDIT	Suspense account		16,000

The correction is therefore:

DEBIT	Suspense account	16,000	
DEBIT	Machinery accumulated depreciation	58,000	
DEBIT	Loss on disposal	6,000	
CREDIT	Machinery cost		80,000

With suspense accounts, you must think carefully about the double entry. Provided you work logically through the following steps, you should be able to tackle these fairly easily.

Step 1 What is the correct entry?

Step 2 What is the actual entry?

Step 3 Prepare the entry needed to correct the error.

Notes

7: Cost of sales and inventories

Topic List

Cost of sales

Accounting for opening and closing inventories

Counting inventories

Measuring inventories

This chapter covers the calculation of cost of sales and the measurement of inventory.

Remember, the inventory figure affects both the statement of financial position and the statement of profit or loss.

| Cost of sales | Accounting for opening and closing inventories | Counting inventories | Measuring inventories |

Formula for the cost of sales

	£
Opening inventory value	X
Add purchases (or production costs)	X
	X
Less closing inventory	(X)
Cost of goods sold	X

Delivery inwards

- Cost paid by purchaser of having goods transported to his business
- Added to cost of purchases

Delivery outwards

- Cost to the seller, paid by the seller, of having goods transported to customer
- Is a selling and distribution expense

Service organisations

Cost of sales for service organisations is based on time incurred on a project/contract.

Only directly attributable costs can be included in the cost of sales for a service organisation.

Ongoing work at year end is recognised in work-in-progress, which is a component of inventories.

| Cost of sales | **Accounting for opening and closing inventories** | Counting inventories | Measuring inventories |

Entries during the year

During the year, purchases are recorded by the following entry:

| DEBIT | Purchases | £ amount bought |
| CREDIT | Cash or payables | £ amount bought |

The inventory account is **not touched at all**.

Entries at year-end

The first thing to do is to transfer the purchases account balance to cost of sales:

| DEBIT | Cost of sales | £ total purchases |
| CREDIT | Purchases | £ total purchases |

The balance on the inventory account is still the **opening inventory** balance. This must also be transferred to cost of sales:

| DEBIT | Cost of sales | £ opening inventory |
| CREDIT | Inventory | £ opening inventory |

The exact reverse entry is made for the **closing inventory** (which will be next year's opening inventory):

| DEBIT | Inventory | £ closing inventory |
| CREDIT | Cost of sales | £ closing inventory |

The year-end entries will be recorded in the adjustments columns when preparing the final trial balance.

| Cost of sales | Accounting for opening and closing inventories | **Counting inventories** | Measuring inventories |

Counting inventories

In order to make the entry for closing inventory, we need to know what is held at the year-end. We find this out **not** from the accounting records, but by going into the warehouse and actually counting the boxes on the shelves.

Inventory drawings

If the owner takes inventory for their own use the entry is:

DEBIT   Drawings
CREDIT Purchases

| Cost of sales | Accounting for opening and closing inventories | Counting inventories | **Measuring inventories** |

Inventory measurement

Measurement

Inventories must be measured at the lower of:

- Cost
- Net realisable value (NRV)

Cost

Can use per IAS 2:

- FIFO or
- Average cost (both periodic weighted average and continuous weighted average)

NRV

Expected selling price	X
Less costs to get items	
ready for sale	(X)
selling costs	(X)
NRV	X

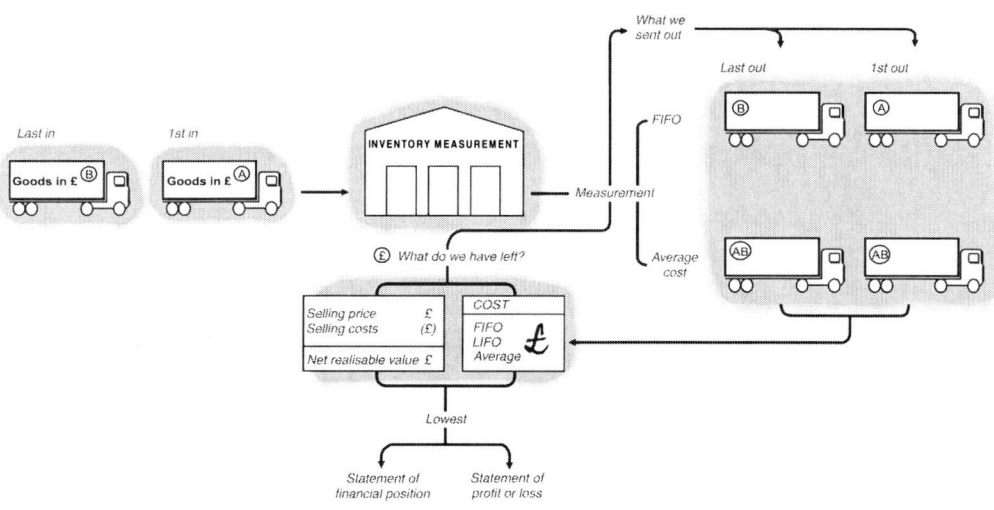

Notes

8: Irrecoverable debts and allowances for receivables

Topic List

Irrecoverable debts and allowances for receivables

Accounting for irrecoverable debts and allowances for receivables

This chapter looks at adjustments that may be required in respect of trade receivables before the financial statements can be prepared.

Irrecoverable debts and allowances for receivables	Accounting for irrecoverable debts and allowances for receivables

Irrecoverable debts and allowances for receivables

A receivable should only be classed as an asset if it is recoverable.

Irrecoverable debts

If definitely irrecoverable, it should be written off to the statement of profit or loss as an irrecoverable debt.

DEBIT Irrecoverable debts expense (SPL)
CREDIT Trade receivables

Allowances for receivables

If uncertainty exists as to the recoverability of trade receivables, an allowance should be set up. This is offset against the receivables balance on the statement of financial position.

DEBIT Irrecoverable debts expense (SPL)
CREDIT Allowance for receivables

| | Irrecoverable debts and allowances for receivables | **Accounting for irrecoverable debts and allowances for receivables** |

Note. Only the **movement** in the allowance for receivables needs to be accounted for.

	£
Allowance required	X
Existing allowance	(X)
Increase/(decrease) required	X/(X)

> If an increase in the allowance for receivables is required, then:
>
> DEBIT   Irrecoverable debts expense (SPL)
> CREDIT Allowance for receivables
>
> If a reduction in the allowance for receivables is required, then:
>
> DEBIT   Allowance for receivables
> CREDIT Irrecoverable debts expense (SPL)

| Irrecoverable debts and allowances for receivables | **Accounting for irrecoverable debts and allowances for receivables** |

Subsequent recovery of debts

If a debt that has previously been written off is subsequently recovered, then:
DEBIT   Trade receivables
CREDIT Irrecoverable debts expense (SPL)

9: Accruals and prepayments

Topic List

Accruals and prepayments

This chapter covers the adjustments which need to be made to expenses in order that the financial statements are prepared in accordance with the accrual accounting principle.

Accruals and prepayments

Accrual

Expenses charged against the profits of a period even though they have not yet been paid for.

Prepayment

Payments made in one period but charged to the later period to which they relate.

Prepayment

Invoice received → **DEBIT** Expenses account
→ **CREDIT** Payables account

Payment made

Part that relates to current accounting period → Expense in SPL

Part that relates to later accounting period → Prepayment. A current asset in the SOFP, not charged as an expense in the SPL.

The amounted debited to the SOFP will hit the SPL in the next period.

Accruals

> Goods or services received
>
> Expense incurred – no invoice yet

Part relating to current accounting period is an accrual.
An acrual is recorded as a current liability in the SPL.

DEBIT SPL
CREDIT SOFP payables (liability)

Accruals and prepayments are **reversed** at the beginning of the next accounting period.

Accruals and prepayments are often entered as adjustments to the trial balance.

> Remember that the financial statements are prepared on an accruals basis and that accruals and prepayments are likely to feature in an accounts preparation question.

Notes

10: Non-current assets and depreciation

Topic List

Tangible non-current assets and depreciation

Depreciation

Tangible non-current asset disposals

Intangible assets

Non-current assets are held by the entity for use over a number of years. Non-current assets are capitalised in the statement of financial position. They are written down over their useful lives by depreciation (tangible assets) or amortisation (intangible assets).

Tangible assets have physical substance and typically include property, machinery and motor vehicles. Intangible assets are also important to many businesses and form part of the non-current assets.

| Tangible non-current assets and depreciation | Depreciation | Tangible non-current asset disposals | Intangible assets |

- Depreciation is a means of allocating the cost of a non-current asset over its expected useful life, so matching cost with revenues earned during that life.

Factors to consider

- Cost of the non-current asset
  - Any amount incurred that is directly attributable to bringing the asset into working condition for its intended use
  - Includes such costs as delivery costs and solicitor's fees incurred relating to the asset's acquisition
- Useful life (to present owner)
- Residual value

Other considerations

- Subsequent expenditure
- Obsolescence

With regard to disclosure, a proforma tangible non-current asset note is shown here.

	Total £'000	Land and buildings £'000	Plant and equipment £'000
Cost or valuation			
At 1 January 20X7	160	100	60
Revaluation surplus	20	20	–
Additions in year	50	30	20
Disposals in year	(45)	(15)	(30)
At 31 December 20X7	185	135	50
Depreciation			
At 1 January 20X7	30	20	10
Charge for year	7	5	2
Eliminated on disposals	(3)	–	(3)
At 31 December 20X7	34	25	9
Carrying amount			
At 31 December 20X7	151	110	41
At 1 January 20X7	130	80	50

| Tangible non-current assets and depreciation | **Depreciation** | Tangible non-current asset disposals | Intangible assets |

Depreciation

A process of matching the original cost of a non-current asset to the accounting periods in which its benefit will be felt.

- Depreciation appears as an expense in the statement of profit or loss. It may be charged annually or monthly, pro rata.
- The annual charges are also accumulated in an accumulated depreciation account in the statement of financial position.
- The credit balance on this account reflects the amount of the asset's original cost which has so far been recognised as an expense.

The annual depreciation charge on a non-current asset is based on two factors.

- The **depreciable amount** of the asset. This is the amount which must be written off over the useful life of the asset. It consists of the original cost less any estimated residual value.
- The **useful life** of the asset. This may be measured in terms of years or in terms of units of service provided by the asset.

If an asset is revalued, the depreciation will be based on the revalued amount and the remaining useful life.

The double entry for depreciation is as follows:

DEBIT   Depreciation expense (SPL)
CREDIT Accumulated depreciation (SOFP)

This reflects:

- A periodic expense in the statement of profit or loss
- A decrease in the asset's carrying amount in the SOFP

Change in expected useful life

- The useful life should be reviewed and changed if no longer appropriate.
- The revised depreciation charge from that date becomes:

$$\frac{\text{Carrying amount at revised date}}{\text{Remaining useful life}}$$

| Tangible non-current assets and depreciation | Depreciation | **Tangible non-current asset disposals** | Intangible assets |

Disposal

On disposal of an asset a profit or loss will arise depending on whether disposal proceeds are greater or less than the carrying amount of the asset.

- If proceeds > Carrying amount = profit
- If proceeds < Carrying amount = loss

Double entry for a disposal

- Eliminate cost
  - DEBIT   Disposals
  - CREDIT   Non-current assets at cost
- Eliminate accumulated depreciation
  - DEBIT   Accumulated depreciation
  - CREDIT   Disposals
- Account for sales proceeds
  - DEBIT   Cash
  - CREDIT   Disposals

  or if part exchange deal
  - DEBIT   Non-current assets
  - CREDIT   Disposals

  with part exchange value
- Transfer balance on disposals account to the statement of profit or loss

| Tangible non-current assets and depreciation | Depreciation | Tangible non-current asset disposals | **Intangible assets** |

Intangible non-current assets

Non-current assets which have a value to the entity but no physical substance, eg, goodwill, patents, licences and development costs.

Development costs

- Research ⟶ All costs written off as incurred
- Development expenditure ⟶ Must be capitalised if certain criteria are met, otherwise are written off

Licences and Patents

- Restrict use by others or give right to operate
- Record at cost less accumulated amortisation

Brands

- Internally generated brands cannot be capitalised
- Purchased brands can be capitalised

Notes

11: Company financial statements

Topic List

Limited liability companies

Shares and dividends

Tax and provisions

Revenue

This section looks at limited liability company accounts.

Limited liability company accounts are more comprehensive than those of sole traders as there are more stakeholders who wish to know how the business is doing.

| Limited liability companies | Shares and dividends | Tax and provisions | Revenue |

Features

Limited liability companies offer limited liability to their owners (shareholders). If the company becomes insolvent, the maximum amount that an owner stands to lose is his share of the capital of the business. This is an attractive prospect to investors. Limited liability companies may be private (Ltd) or public (plc). IAS 1 sets out a suggested format for financial statements.

- Owners = shareholders or members
- Large number of owners
- Owner/manager split
- Owners appoint directors to run business on their behalf
- Owners receive share of profits in form of dividends

Disadvantages

- Compliance with national legislation
- Compliance with national accounting standards and/or IFRS Accounting Standards
- Any formation or annual registration costs

Funding

Companies are funded in the following ways:

- Retained profits
- Short-term liabilities (trade payables etc)
- Share capital
- Loan notes

| Limited liability companies | **Shares and dividends** | Tax and provisions | Revenue |

Shares

The proprietors' capital in a limited liability company consists of share capital. When a company is set up for the first time it issues shares, which are paid for by investors, who then become shareholders of the company.

Shares are denominated in units of 25 pence, 50 pence, £1 or whatever seems appropriate. This is referred to as their nominal value.

Preference shares

- Rights depend on articles
- Right to fixed dividend with priority over ordinary shares
- Do not usually carry voting rights
- Generally priority for capital in winding up
- May be cumulative or non-cumulative

Ordinary shares

- No right to fixed dividend
- Entitled to remaining profits after preferred dividend
- Entitled to surplus on repayment of capital

| Limited liability companies | **Shares and dividends** | Tax and provisions | Revenue |

Preference shares

Preference shares can be redeemable or irredeemable.

Redeemable preference shares	**Irredeemable preference shares**
Treated as debt, not share capital, and therefore classified as liabilities.	Treated as equity and therefore included in the equity section of the SOFP.
Dividends on redeemable preference shares are treated as finance costs.	Dividends are deducted from retained earnings.

In the exam you will be told whether preference shares are redeemable or irredeemable and can assume that irredeemable preference shares are equity and redeemable preference shares are debt.

Share capital

- **Issued.** The amount of share capital that has been issued to shareholders.
- **Nominal value.** The amount at which each share is initially issued.
- **Market value.** This is the price at which someone is prepared to purchase the share from an existing shareholder. It is different from nominal value.

The following are the main types of share issue:

- New issue at par or at a premium
- Rights issue
- Bonus issue

Rights issue

A rights issue of shares is made to existing owners in proportion to their shareholdings.

Bonus issue

A bonus issue is a free issue of shares to existing shareholders. Amounts from retained earnings and share premium may be reclassified as share capital in a bonus issue.

| Limited liability companies | **Shares and dividends** | Tax and provisions | Revenue |

Loan notes

Companies may issue loan notes. These are long term liabilities not capital. They differ from shares as follows:

- Shareholder = owner; noteholder = payable
- Loan note interest **must** be paid; not so dividends
- Loan notes often secured on company assets

Reserves

Revenue reserves consist of distributable profits and can be paid out as dividends.

- Retained earnings
- Others, as the directors decide

Capital reserves are not available for distribution.

- **Share premium.** The Companies Act 2006 requires that whenever shares are issued for a consideration in excess of their nominal value such a premium shall be credited to a share premium account.
- For the purposes of *Accounting Fundamentals*, the share premium account can be used to issue bonus shares.

Dividends

Equity dividends

An equity (or ordinary) share entitles its holder to dividends which vary in amount depending on the performance and policy of the company.

It is recorded as:

DEBIT   Retained earnings
CREDIT Cash at bank/dividend payable *

* The credit depends on whether the dividend was paid in the year or is outstanding at year end.

Preference dividends

A preference share entitles the holder to a fixed dividend, whose payment takes priority over that of ordinary share dividends. How preference dividend is accounted for depends on whether the preference share is classified as debt (redeemable) or equity (irredeemable).

If classified as debt:

DEBIT   Finance cost (SPL)
CREDIT Cash at bank / dividend payable

If classified as equity:

Record as per equity dividends above

| Limited liability companies | Shares and dividends | **Tax and provisions** | Revenue |

Tax

Companies pay income tax on their profits. The charge may not be due for payment until after the year end, so there will be a taxation payable balance included under current liabilities in the statement of financial position.

Provisions

A provision is a liability of uncertain timing or amount. Provisions involve a degree of **estimation** because the exact amount of the liability cannot be reliably measured.

Accounting for tax

Tax payable on the profits for the accounting period will be posted as follows:

DEBIT   Income tax expense
CREDIT   Tax payable (current liabilities)

Accounting for provisions

To create a provision:

DEBIT   Expenses
CREDIT   Provisions (current liabilities)

Revenue

- Revenue includes credit and cash sales (net of discounts), refunds and VAT.
- Revenue should be recognised when control of the goods and services is transferred from the supplier to the customer.
- Revenue is income arising in the ordinary course of an entity's activities.

IFRS 15 applies the following process to determining whether revenue can be recognised:

- Identify the contract with the customer.
- Identify the separate performance obligations.
- Determine the transaction price.
- Allocate the transaction price to the performance obligations.
- Recognise revenue when (or as) a performance obligation is satisfied.

Notes

12: Company financial statements under IFRS Accounting Standards

Topic List

IAS 1

This section looks at limited company accounts prepared under IFRS Accounting Standards.

It builds on the knowledge from Chapter 11 as well as previous chapters, and helps you to prepare financial statements in accordance with IAS 1.

IAS 1

ABC Co
Statement of financial position as at December 20X2

	20X2 £	20X2 £	20X1 £	20X1 £
ASSETS				
Non-current assets				
Property, plant and equipment	X		X	
Intangible assets	X		X	
		X		X
Current assets				
Inventories	X		X	
Trade receivables	X		X	
Other current assets	X		X	
Cash and cash equivalents	X		X	
		X		X
Total assets		X		X

ABC Co
Statement of financial position as at December 20X2 (cont)

	20X2 $	20X1 $
EQUITY AND LIABILITIES		
Equity		
Share capital	X	X
Retained earnings/(losses)	X	X
Other components of equity	X	X
Total equity	X	X
Non-current liabilities		
Long-term borrowings	X	X
Provisions	X	X
	X	X
Current liabilities		
Trade and other payables	X	X
Short-term borrowings	X	X
Current portion of long-term borrowings	X	X
Provisions	X	X
Current tax payable	X	X
	X	X
Total equity and liabilities	X	X

IAS 1

ABC Co
Statement of profit or loss for the year ended 31 December 20X2

	20X2	20X1
	£	£
Revenue	X	X
Cost of sales	(X)	(X)
Gross profit	X	X
Other income	X	X
Distribution costs	(X)	(X)
Administrative expenses	(X)	(X)
Other expenses	(X)	(X)
Investment income	X	X
Finance cost	(X)	(X)
Profit before tax	X	X
Income tax expense	(X)	(X)
Profit for the year	X	X

ABC Co
Statement of changes in equity for the year ended 31 December 20X2

	Share capital	Retained earnings	Other reserves	Total
	£	£	£	£
Balance as at 1 January 20X2	X	X	X	X
Issue of share capital	X			X
Dividends		(X)		(X)
Profit/(loss) for the year		X		X
Balance as at 31 December 20X2	X	X	X	X

Notes

13: Company financial statements under UK GAAP

Topic List

UK GAAP

Published accounts

Terminology

Balance sheet and P&L

Here we look at financial statements under UK GAAP.

Note the formats of the profit and loss account and balance sheet.

| UK GAAP | Published accounts | Terminology | Balance sheet and P&L |

UK GAAP

The rules, from whatever source, that govern accounting and financial reporting in the UK.

Constituents

- Company law (the Companies Act 2006)
- UK accounting standards
- The effects of stock exchange listing requirements (which apply directly to listed companies but which are influential more widely)
- The effects of international accounting and financial reporting standards

GAAP is a dynamic concept: it changes constantly as circumstances alter through new legislation, standards and practice.

Statutory accounts

Financial statements which limited companies are obliged by law to publish in a particular form.

Under UK GAAP the accounts must include:

- A profit and loss account (equivalent to a statement of profit or loss)
- A balance sheet as at the date to which the profit and loss account is made up (equivalent to a statement of financial position)
- A directors' report, and a directors' remuneration report in the case of a quoted company
- An auditors' report addressed to the members (not to the directors) of the company

| UK GAAP | **Published accounts** | Terminology | Balance sheet and P&L |

True and fair view

The Companies Act 2006 requirement that the accounts show a true and fair view is paramount.

Listed companies

Produce a statement of profit or loss and statement of financial position following international terminology and formats.

Non-listed companies

Can choose between UK GAAP or international terminology and formats for their published accounts.

Terminology

UK GAAP uses different terminology in financial statements:

International term	UK GAAP term
Statement of profit or loss	Profit and loss account or Income statement
Statement of financial position	Balance sheet
Non-current asset	Fixed asset
International term	Property, plant and equipment
UK GAAP term	Tangible fixed assets
Carrying amount	Net book value
Inventories	Stock
Receivables	Debtors
Irrecoverable debt	Bad debt

Irrecoverable debt expense	Bad and doubtful debts expense
Allowance for receivables	Allowance for doubtful debts
Retained earnings	Retained profits (reserve)
Payables	Creditors
Non-current liabilities	Creditors: amounts falling due after more than one year
Current liabilities	Creditors: amounts falling due in less than one year
Revenue	Turnover
Finance costs	Interest expense

| | UK GAAP | Published accounts | Terminology | **Balance sheet and P&L** |

Typical company limited balance sheet as at ….

	£	£	£
Fixed assets			
Intangible assets			
Development costs	X		
Patents, licences, trademarks	X		
Goodwill	X		
		X	
Tangible assets			
Land and buildings	X		
Plant and machinery	X		
Fixtures, fittings, tools and equipment	X		
Motor vehicles	X		
		X	
			X
Current assets			
Stocks	X		
Debtors and prepayments	X		
Cash at bank and in hand	X		
		X	
Creditors: amounts falling due within one year (ie, current liabilities)			
Debenture loans (nearing their redemption date)	X		
Bank overdraft and loans	X		
Trade creditors	X		
Taxation	X		
Accruals	X		
		(X)	

	£	£	£
NET CURRENT ASSETS			X
Total assets less current liabilities			X
Creditors: amounts falling due after more than one year			
Debenture loans			(X)
			――
			X
			══

Capital and reserves
Called up share capital
Ordinary shares   X
Preference shares   X
                                            ――
                                             X

Reserves
Share premium   X
Other reserves   X
Profit and loss account (retained profits) X
                                ――
                                 X
                                ══

	UK GAAP	Published accounts	Terminology	**Balance sheet and P&L**

**Typical company limited
Profit and loss account
for the year ended…**

	£	£
Turnover		X
Cost of sales		(X)
Gross profit		X
Distribution costs	X	
Administrative expenses	(X)	
		(X)
Operating profit		X
Other operating income		X
Interest payable		(X)
Profit before tax		X
Tax		(X)
Profit after tax		X

14: Sole trader and partnership financial statements under UK GAAP

Topic List

The balance sheet

The profit and loss account

Partnership accounts

This chapter deals with UK GAAP accounts for sole traders and partnerships..

| | The balance sheet | The profit and loss account | Partnership accounts |

The balance sheet

A list of assets, liabilities and capital of a business at a given moment.

Jedster
Balance sheet as at 31 August 20X1

	£	£
Fixed assets		
Freehold premises		100,000
Fixtures and fittings		16,000
Motor vehicles		18,000
		134,000
Current assets		
Stocks	10,000	
Debtors	23,000	
Cash	800	
	33,800	

Current liabilities		
Bank overdraft	4,000	
Creditors	3,600	
Taxation payable	7,000	
	14,600	
Net current assets		19,200
		153,200
Long-term liabilities		
Loan		(50,000)
Net assets		103,200
Capital		
Capital as at 1 September 20X0		95,200
Profit for the year		16,000
		111,200
Less drawings		(8,000)
Capital as at 31 August 20X1		103,200

▸ Net current assets = working capital

▸ Net assets = assets – liabilities

Note that **share capital** in limited company accounts is replaced by the sole trader's capital balance, plus profit for the year, less drawings.

| The balance sheet | **The profit and loss account** | Partnership accounts |

The profit and loss account

Matches revenue earned in a period with the costs incurred in earning it

Jedster – Profit and loss account for the year ended 31 August 20X1

	£	£
Sales		80,000
Opening stock	5,000	
Purchases	40,000	
Closing stock	(10,000)	
Cost of sales		35,000
Gross profit		45,000
Less expenses		
Rent	12,000	
Depreciation	41,000	
Wages	12,000	
Other expenses	4,000	
		29,000
Net Profit		**16,000**

Gross profit = sales – cost of sales

Gross profit margin = $\frac{45,000}{80,000} \times 100\% = 56.25\%$

Net profit = gross profit – expenses

Note that income tax is not included in sole trader accounts.

| | The balance sheet | The profit and loss account | **Partnership accounts** |

Partnership agreement

A partnership is an arrangement between two or more individuals in which they undertake to share the risks and rewards of a joint business operations.

The financial arrangements agreed between the partners are often set out in a format document called a **partnership agreeement**.

If there is no aggreement, Partnership Act 1980 applies.

Advantages of partnership

Partnership v sole trader.
- Spread risk
- Network of contacts
- Partners being in business, skills and experience
- Easier to raise finance

Partnership v limited company.
- No need to comply with statutory requirements such as audit
- No need to comply with accounting standards
- No formation or registration fees

However, note the following disadvantages

- Profits spead
- Dilution of control
- Disputes between partners

- No limited liability

| The balance sheet | The profit and loss account | **Partnership accounts** |

Capital and current accounts

It is usual to maintain both a capital account and a current account for each partner.

A partner's capital account shows any cash or other assets brought by them into the business. They will usually make an initial capital construction when they join the partnership, but there may also be further injections (or withdrawals) of capital later on.

White the balance on a partner's capital account is likely to remain stable for lone periods, their current account balance will fluctuate more rapidly.

- They will draw money regulary from the business to support their living expenses and these drawings will be debts to his current account.
- They will be entitled to a share of the business profits and this will be credited to their current account at least annually.

PROFORMA CURRENT ACCOUNT

	X	Y	Z		X	Y	Z
	£	£	£		£	£	£
Drawings	X	X	X	Profit share	X	X	X
Balance c/f	X	X	X		X	X	X
	X	X	X				

Appropriation accounts

In the case of a sole trader, retained profits earned each year are simply added to his capital balance. With a partnership things are more complicated.

After calculating the net profit earned by the business an appropriation statement must be prepared to determine the allocation of profit between the partners.

The sum available for appropriation must now be shared amongst the partners and credited to their current accounts in accordance with the profit sharing ratio.

Notes

Notes